A New True Book

THE ANASAZI

By David Petersen

CHILDRENS PRESS ®

CHICAGO

The Zuni pueblo people are
descendants of the Anasazi.

PHOTO CREDITS
© Reinhard Brucker—6, 7, 8 (2 photos),
10 (3 photos), 12, 13 (2 photos), 14, 16,
19, 20 (bottom), 25 (right), 27, 28, 31, 32,
34, 39, 40 (bottom), 43 (4 photos), 44
Cameramann International Ltd.—4, 5
North Wind Picture Archives—17, 25
(left), 36
Photri—© Ernesto Burciaga, 20 (top)
© Carl Purcell—Cover
Root Resources—© Stephen Trimble, 38
© John Running—42 (2 photos)
TSW-CLICK/Chicago—© Robert Frerck,
2; © Ken Gallard, 23; © Bill Gillette, 40
(top); © Marie Ueda, 45
Cover—Cliff dwelling, Mesa Verde,
      Colorado

Library of Congress Cataloging-in-Publication Data

Petersen, David
   The Anasazi / by David Petersen
      p.   cm. — (A New true book)
   Includes index.
   Summary: Describes the homes, culture, and way of
life of the Anasazi, the Ancient Ones of the
southwestern United States whose descendants
became the Pueblos.
   ISBN 0-516-01121-9
   1. Pueblo Indians—Antiquities—Juvenile literature.
2. Southwest, New—Antiquities—Juvenile literature.
[1. Pueblo Indians—Antiquities. 2. Indians of
North America—Southwest, New—Antiquities.
3. Southwest, New—Antiquities.] I. Title.
E99.P9P415 1991   91-3036
979'.01—dc20   CIP
                                         AC

TABLE OF CONTENTS

A marker shows the point where the four states
of Arizona, Utah, Colorado, and New Mexico meet.

THE ANCIENT ONES

There is a place in the American Southwest where the corners of four states touch. These states are Arizona, Colorado, Utah, and New Mexico. This place is called the Four Corners.

The Four Corners is the only place in the United States where four states meet.

Canyon de Chelly is in Arizona near the Four Corners region.

Most of the land in the
Four Corners region is like
a desert. There are lots of
flat-topped mountains
called mesas, and many
deep canyons.

About two thousand years ago, a group of Native American people moved into the Four Corners region. They learned to survive in the harsh land, and for more

The Anasazi carved these pictures on rocks hundreds of years ago.

Anasazi pottery (left), covered with black-and-white designs. The flat stone (right) was used to sharpen axes.

than a thousand years, they thrived there. Then they simply disappeared.

Today, we call these people the *Anasazi*—a Navajo Indian word meaning "the Ancient Ones."

Nobody knows what the Anasazi called themselves. But, like most Native Americans, their name for themselves probably meant "the People."

Scientists have studied their skeletons and mummies, so we know what the Anasazi looked like. We know they were short and stocky. Their hair was usually long and black, but some Anasazi had brown, wavy hair.

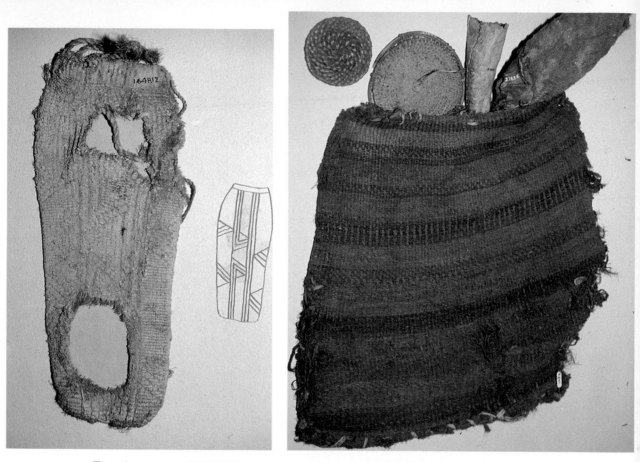

The Anasazi
Basket Makers
made sandals (above)
and containers (above
right) from
plant fibers.
The Basket Makers
were named for
their beautiful
baskets (right).

10

THE BASKET MAKERS

The earliest Anasazi lived in the Four Corners region for about seven hundred years. We call them the Basket Makers because they wove beautiful baskets and sandals from tree bark and plant fibers.

The first Basket Makers got most of their food by hunting and gathering.

The men and boys used nets for catching rabbits and spears for hunting larger animals—deer, bison, and wild sheep.

The Anasazi drew pictures of the animals that they hunted.

The Anasazi traded with the people of Mexico for copper bells (left). At the right are an Anasazi ax, a clay pot, and shell bracelets.

The women and girls gathered roots, cactus flowers, pine nuts, and plants.

Because the early Basket Makers moved around a lot, they had no real houses. Sometimes,

13

they made crude brush shelters. But most of the time, they camped in caves.

Later, the Basket Makers became farmers. They grew corn, squash, and beans. They also kept turkeys, weaving their feathers into warm blankets.

Anasazi pottery and woven blankets.
The blanket hanging at the right is made of turkey feathers.

As farmers, the Basket Makers began to build houses and stay in one place. They no longer had to move constantly to find food.

The homes they built were pit houses made of tree branches and dirt. They dug large, round holes a few feet deep. Over the holes, the Basket Makers built slanted walls and flat roofs, using tree limbs, bark, and earth.

Usually, one large family lived in each pit house.

For cooking and heat, there was a fireplace in the center of the floor. An opening in the roof let the smoke out. A ladder down through the smoke hole was used to enter and leave the pit house.

Inside a pit house. The wooden ladder leads up to ground level.

THE PUEBLO ANASAZI

About thirteen hundred
years ago, the Anasazi
discovered the bow and
arrow. This weapon could
shoot farther and straighter
than the spear. They also

The bow and arrow helped hunters kill more animals for food.

learned to make pottery
and they traded with other
Indians for cotton.

The Anasazi began
building their houses
above the ground. First,
they made a framework of
tree limbs and bark. Then
they covered it with a
thick coating of mud,
called adobe. When the
adobe dried, it was hard
and waterproof.

An Anasazi stone wall. The adobe between the stones
has disappeared after centuries of weathering.

Later, the Anasazi learned
to build houses by stacking
up blocks of sandstone,
like big bricks. They used
adobe to cement the blocks

19

The ruins of
Anasazi buildings
are found
throughout the
Four Corners region.

together. The ruins of
thousands of these Anasazi
buildings still stand
throughout the Four
Corners region.

In time, the people
began to build their
houses together to form
pueblos. We call these
people the Pueblo Anasazi.

Many pueblos were built
on the open mesas. But

the most amazing Anasazi
pueblos were built in
caves high on the sides of
cliffs. The Anasazi used
ladders and ropes to get
up and down the steep
cliffs. Also, shallow finger
and toe holds were cut
into the rock.

Opposite page: A famous Anasazi cliff ruin is located
in Mesa Verde National Park in Colorado.

ANASAZI DAILY LIFE

Anasazi babies were carried around on their mothers' backs, strapped into a backboard.

There were no schools. Young children learned by helping their parents.

Girls helped their mothers carry water, grind corn, weave baskets, and make pottery. They also learned to prepare meals and keep house.

The Anasazi had to carry water up to their pueblos which were built on the tops of mesas (left). Stones (right) were used for grinding corn.

Boys helped their fathers in the cornfields. Later they went with the men on hunting trips.

In summer, both men and women wore skirts woven from cotton or

yucca fibers. Young
children often wore no
clothes. In winter, young
and old wore blankets and
robes made of rabbit skins
or turkey feathers.

Anasazi pueblos had
open courts called plazas.
The women and girls sat
in the plaza and talked
while they worked. Young
children played, and the
dogs and turkeys ran free

This Anasazi pueblo ruin in Mesa Verde National Park is called the Long House Ruin.

in the plaza. On special holidays, all the people gathered there to sing, dance, and feast.

The ruin of a kiva at Mesa Verde. The large hole in the floor is the fireplace. The small hole is the *sipapu*, or spirit hole.

Underground, beneath the plazas, the Anasazi built rooms called *kivas*. Like the old pit house of the Basket Makers, the kiva was round, with a fireplace in the center of the floor, and a smoke hole in the roof. But the kiva also had a *sipapu*, or spirit hole in the floor. It represented the opening through which the Anasazi believed the first people entered the world.

Down in the dark, smoky kivas, the Anasazi men gathered to work, talk, sing, and perform religious ceremonies.

The Anasazi led hard lives. The cliffs on which many of their pueblos were perched are high and steep. The Four Corners winters are cold, and the summers very hot.

A cliff pueblo in New Mexico. Note the
ladder that leads to the cliff top.

And if the summer rains
didn't come, the crops
might fail. Then the people
would starve.

But Anasazi life could
be a good life. Scientists

Anasazi clay pots and hunting arrows

believe the Anasazi were
happy and healthy people.
They were intelligent.
They had strong houses.
They made beautiful
pottery. And they enjoyed
themselves.

ANASAZI MYSTERIES

More than seven hundred years ago—two hundred years before the first Europeans came to America—the Anasazi disappeared from the Four Corners area.

This Anasazi ruin at Mesa Verde is called the Cliff Palace.

They left their beautiful pueblos. Why?

Nobody knows what happened. They may have

left because their water

supply dried up. Scientists know that there was a drought about seven hundred fifty years ago that lasted twenty-four years.

Without water, the Anasazi could not grow their crops. They could not make adobe for their houses. They could not even make pottery.

An artist's drawing of an attack on an Anasazi pueblo

The Anasazi might have been attacked by other tribes. That is probably why they built their pueblos on the dangerous cliffs to begin with. There, they could defend themselves from attackers.

Finally, by the time the Pueblo Anasazi left, it is possible that they had used most of the area's natural resources. The hunters may have killed most of the animals. Most of the trees may have been cut down for lumber and firewood. And perhaps

the soil lost its richness.
Then crops could no
longer grow.

But all we know for
certain is that the Anasazi
left.

WHERE DID THE ANASAZI GO?

They wandered south.
Some settled along the
Rio Grande River Valley
between Albuquerque and
Santa Fe in New Mexico.

The Rio Grande River and the Sandia Mountains in New Mexico

Zuni women (above) in traditional dress. The Hopi man below is carving kachina dolls.

Others went to the Zuni
and Hopi pueblos of
Arizona.

In these new places the
Anasazi found water, rich
soil, trees, and friendly
Indians. Over the centuries,
the Anasazi and their new
neighbors became one
people.

The Pueblo peoples of today keep many of the traditions that began with the Anasazi.

Today's Hopi and Zuni people of Arizona, and the Pueblo tribes of New Mexico, are the descendants of the Anasazi—the Ancient Ones.

42

The Hopi pottery and baskets of today are like those made by their ancestors, the Anasazi. A kachina doll (above) is used in Hopi religious ceremonies.

They still live in adobe houses. They still raise corn, beans, and squash. They still make beautiful pottery. And they still use kivas for their traditional religious ceremonies.

Ruins of an Anasazi kiva at Chaco Canyon, New Mexico

In all these ways, the
Ancient Ones live on.
Maybe someday you will
visit an Anasazi ruin. If you

Anasazi ruins at Mesa Verde

do, look around and think
of the people who once
lived there. The people are
gone, but their way of life
remains strong.

WORDS YOU SHOULD KNOW

adobe (uh • DOH • bee) — a heavy clay found in desert regions

Anasazi (an • uh • SAH • zee) — the people who lived in the Four Corners area of the American Southwest until about seven hundred years ago

ancient (AIN • shint) — very old

bison (BY • sun) — a large hoofed animal with short horns and a humped back; often called a buffalo

canyon (KAN • yun) — a long, narrow valley that has high cliffs on each side

ceremony (SAIR • ih • mo • nee) — a celebration or a religious service

constantly (KAHN • stint • lee) — never stopping; going on all the time

desert (DEH • zert) — an area of land that gets little rainfall and has very dry soil

drought (DROWT) — a lack of normal rainfall over a period of months or years

fibers (FYE • berz) — tough, stringy plant parts

fireplace (FY • er • plaiss) — a place inside a house where a fire is made, lined with stones or other fireproof materials

kiva (KEE • va) — an underground room used for ceremonies by Indian people in the southwestern United States

mesa (MAY • sa) — a high, rocky hill having steep sides and a flat top

mummies (MUM • eez) — the remains of human bodies that have been preserved by being dried out

pit (PIT) — a deep hole in the ground

plaza (PLAH • za) — an open area in a town or city

pottery (PAHT • er • ee) — cups, bowls, etc., formed of clay and dried until it hardens

pueblo (PWEB • lo) — a Spanish word for "town" or "village"

region (REE • jun) — a large area of a country

resources (REE • sor • sez) — supplies of materials such as water or wood, used to take care of people's needs

ruin (ROO • in) — the remains of buildings that have decayed or been destroyed

sandstone (SAND • stohn) — a soft stone formed from sand that has been put under great pressure inside the earth

sipapu (sih • PAH • poo) — a hole in the roof of a kiva

stocky (STAH • kee) — having a heavy build

thrive (THRYVE) — to grow strong and healthy

yucca (YUCK • ah) — a tall plant with long, stiff leaves that grows in dry places

INDEX

About the Author

David Petersen is a freelance writer and the author of Among the Elk *(Northland Publishing Company, 1988). He lives in Colorado and has written many titles in the New True Book series.*